Timothy Forse

FOR THE JOURNEY

Copyright © 2018 Tim Forse

All rights reserved.

ISBN:1987792963
ISBN-13:9781987792966

Timothy Forse

FOR THE JOURNEY

Poetic Reflections of a traveller

To C, L & P.

Deo Gratias

2018

FOR THE JOURNEY

CONTENTS

1	For the Journey	1
2	Solo Train Travel	3
3	The Traveller	5
4	Late May Day Bank Holiday	8
5	Caffe Excelsior	10
6	The Way to Islay	12
7	The Commuter	13
8	Journey by Sea	14
9	Journey by Air	16
10	Journey of Life	18
11	Journey to Heaven	20
	About the author	23

For the Journey

All have to travel
Some do it by train
Sometimes a few feet
Are all that remain.

From first breath
To last release
None of us can
Avoid decease.

So with happiness
And gladness of heart
I revisit the Terminus
To depart.

The point of arrival
Where hot and tired
I long ago sought
A wash and a bed.

Much wiser now
I plan matters better
A friend collects
Me for Dinner.

I depart refreshed
Restored, content,
To be greeted
At the other end.

It suddenly is summer
Outside in the heat
And in my heart
I sense the sweet.

Surprise is alive
The long known place
Revisited now
Has novelty.

It is now
We know
We follow
And yet

Our task
Is to go
Where none
Have gone

And how odd
In saying less
We find life more
Close to God.

Andermatt to Milan to Trent August 2017

FOR THE JOURNEY

Solo Train Travel

The joy of the train

Is constant change

As the I sits still

The mind can range.

Little interruptions

Neighbours angst or bliss

Add life to the aloneness.

There is novelty in this.

The time of departure

Is a source of derision

Frozen points and leaves

Interfere with precision.

The destination chosen

May not be the end

Either of the line

Or finding a friend.

Our destiny is related

To another dimension

We sense in our heart

This is more than a station.

Time flies as we travel

From wherever we depart

We can find him at the end

No matter when we start.

FOR THE JOURNEY

The Traveller

Many have the wanderlust

Always longing for new places

Be they mountains or desert dust

Seas, lakes or urban spaces.

I am no longer exceptional

In travelling far and wide.

The difference is generational

Work required it, I complied.

I listen more to friends now

Who eulogise on the exotic

A few must trek by eternal snow

Others visit things historic.

When young I listened to my elders

Speaking restrainedly of foreign lands

Never of pain and loss in warfare

Just of the goodness of their friends.

Their actions were their teaching

Taking me to sombre sites

Not to churches to hear preaching

Just to the relics of their plight.

Then with joy we went to mountains

Where we grew in strength and skills

Racing downhill stretched our sinews

And made us hungry for new thrills.

There was great happiness and laughter

That seemed like heaven to me

And school and sport thereafter

Not my thing nor fancy free.

Doing my best was what I did

Or so I thought, and then I hid

My inner fears of falling short

Above all the fear of being caught.

FOR THE JOURNEY

A wise friend said "protect yourself"

I could not see, I lost good health

Worn out working at making wealth

With not enough space for Grace.

Then came a gentle loving word,

I heard "you do too much"

"Here is reality in all totality."

Peace is complete in such.

Late May Day Bank Holiday

The sun shines well

And weddings tell

This is the happy

Time of the year.

That is suddenly

Clear from the fun

Of friendships begun

With love on their faces.

Trainloads travel

To joyful places

And yet the news

Seems dire.

Metaphor can

Be killed

By Reason.

And yet it is

FOR THE JOURNEY

As if the Mayflower

Has just sailed back

To England.

Paradox finds

At such times

In human hearts

A refoundland.

And when I smile

At such encounters

A new song begins

In mine.

The way

To Heaven

Is through sin

Forgiven.

Caffe Excelsior.

I sat where you had a Schweppes

And I a cappuccino

Where later we stood to greet

On St Peter's Street

Another chapter begins

New school for you

Fresh start for me

Soon in September.

That was tomorrow.

The challenges described

Faced with no fear

Timidity banished.

There may be moments

When it attempts to return,

What indecision permits

Clear action prevents.

FOR THE JOURNEY

In a world where sin

Is largely replaced

By valid experience

Faith in the I matters more.

Conscience develops

As we learn to be hurt

Goodness demands

Do not wound others.

As we travel each day

We grow to our destiny

This does not show

Unless far falling or rising.

If we sense a decline

When in fact we are rising

We are missing the point -

Sudden joy is surprising.

The Way to Islay

You flew separately from the South.
The confirming text of Boarding
Came as I drove by Lindisfarne
Holiness of meeting bringing.

And so together we left Edinburgh.
We needed the Motorway to make it
To Clydeside then the winding road
Up hills and down till the ship we found.

Time to the Isles is far from certain,
Storms can shut ferries; we found fine weather,
Calm crossings, clear lochs, iced mountains,
And joyful eating together.

Distilleries visited, whiskies tasted
The driver sober, guests elated
"The sofa beckons" so said our friend
As we sail homeward toward journey's end.

FOR THE JOURNEY

The Commuter

Commuters are people

Who daily exchange

Among a wide range

Their place of work and sleep.

It is frequently thought

To involve mainly a train

For the select, sometimes a plane.

For more, a car, bus, bike or foot.

The other meaning

And type of exchange

Is at Law it can commute

Death for reprieve.

Commuting by moving

Consumes in different degrees.

Commuting in law provides

Just forgiveness for pleas.

Journey by Sea

The boat journey to Europe is brief

Across the busiest lane in the world

And at this narrow point where ships could collide

They don't.

Navigation has now reduced the risk

Of damage or loss to be negligible.

Skilled use of radar, compass and charts

Have developed so this is made possible.

Still every sailor respects the sea

As larger than them with storms and shocks,

And can learn from heroic Odysseus

Who avoided the sirens and rocks.

Though contemporary risks seem slight

May we like Odysseus

Return without shipwreck

From every Voyage or Flight.

FOR THE JOURNEY

The voyage of life is like this

For all through thick and thin.

Or as Clement the Great once put it

"Journeying through waves of sin."

True vision to guide our journey

Is like Odysseus coming home to Penelope.

We can all take wrong turnings

And a lifetime of learning

To find a peaceful haven as destiny.

Journey by Air

When visiting friends

Arrive by air

We take more notice

Of this affair.

Such a journey

Is worthy of attention

As it indicates

A caring action.

More people make effort

To come and greet

Guests on arrival

Its a joy to meet.

When they depart

It is a loving thing

Leaving them for a flight,

A sign of the heart.

FOR THE JOURNEY

Be assured

When he comes again

It is likely

It will be by plane.

Journey of Life

None of us can

Choose our birthplace

Whatever our nation,

Faith or race.

Our place of beginning

Belongs to others

Generally our fathers

And always our mothers.

Some may have no father

Present or extant

Others have him

Not too distant.

From then we may cry

To determine our destiny

And as soon as we grow

We may go where we say.

FOR THE JOURNEY

By choosing our own Way

We can make many mistakes

Listening to loved ones

Happiness makes.

And if we still fall,

On meeting the Other

In no time at all

We quickly recover.

And so to our destiny

In love for eternity.

Providing we believe

It is Heaven we achieve

By shunning the nothingness

Of material modernity.

Journey to Heaven

Green fields glistened

Near ripe white wheat waved

By the line

As I took the train.

She is there already

I sensed

Ahead of us

Free from pain.

Laughter of the passengers

On the bus

Indicated joy not fear

And just as she would wish

No fuss.

FOR THE JOURNEY

"She had a good innings"

The vicar said

When great aunt died

And she made eighty five

In the same place

Somehow ninety six

Seemed no different

For Peg.

I told her grandson

How good she was

And had held me at the Font

When just thirty and I not one.

The service began

With the Lark Ascending

And ended coffin touching

As Bocelli sang.

She seems now somehow

More lively in love

The gentle voice of care

Expresses it still.

Now in the eternal

Beyond the numbers

Of age and place

There seems a richer way.

I paused and smelt

The yellow rose's scent

In the garden, just there

By the path to Heaven.

ABOUT THE AUTHOR

This is Tim Forse's second collection of Poetic reflections.

He has drawn his inspiration from a Community of Understanding of young people notably those belonging to the Communion and Liberation movement founded by Luigi Giussani.

His working life has involved fairly constant travel. This collection aims to relate physical travel to the journey through life.

It is rooted in his sacramental experience of being a regular communicant and the renewal process he has found in that.

The way he finds faith to illuminate reason is at one with the exposition provided by Luigi Giussani, and provides a path of understanding at once catholic and reformed.

Made in the USA
Columbia, SC
18 September 2018